GARDEN PARTY

Grandmother's Flower Garden Quilts and More

Dorothy Kinsley Wray

DEDICATION

To our daughters Joann and Rosemary, and their families, for their unconditional love and support.

ACKNOWLEDGEMENTS

My thanks to Helen Frost whose editing was invaluable. And heartfelt thanks to my husband, Robert, for standing behind me, for never complaining about the fabric I buy, for helping with quilt shows, for making quilt labels, and now for helping with cutting and quilting and even my housework - how could I ask any more of him.

Illustrations by Helen Frost

Photography by David Elliott
Tucson, Arizona

Typesetting by Digi-Pix
Tucson, Arizona

Printed by Arizona Lithographers
Tucson, Arizona

Published by First Star
10237 East Rio de Oro
Tucson, Arizona 85749
(520) 885-7278

ISBN: 0-9633917-4-7

CONTENTS

FOREWORD

by Helen Frost

A hundred hexagon quilts? The thought was overwhelming and just a little bit unbelievable. Yet that's what the letter, in Quilters' Newsletter Magazine's Quilting Bee, very clearly stated. Since Dorothy Wray, the author of the letter and the maker of those hundred quilts, lived in Arizona as I do, an introductory phone call was soon followed by a visit.

At the time, Dorothy and her husband Robert were spending the winter months in the mild, dry climate of Quartzsite, Arizona. As the name implies, the town and surrounding area is rich in rocks and minerals and is home to the largest gem and mineral show in the country. While Dorothy showed me quilt after quilt, Robert entertained my husband and children with his extensive knowledge of rocks.

A native of Kansas, Dorothy met and married Robert in California. Most of their married life has been spent in Tahoe City, California, across the lake from Lake Tahoe, Nevada. There they raised their two daughters while establishing a successful hardware store and a heavy equipment sales and rental business.

They had great plans for their retirement, starting in 1973. Traveling in a motor home, they planned to explore the United States, with many hours of fishing anticipated by Robert. Dorothy remembers, "Everybody was concerned about what I was going to do, how I was going to keep my hands busy." A chance visit to an antique store supplied the answer, and the beginning of an incredible quiltmaking career.

Draped over a table in the store was a Grandmother's Flower Garden quilt. Although at that time Dorothy had not yet made a quilt, the pattern was a familiar one. All of Dorothy's older sisters, prior to their weddings in the 1920s and '30s, were given Flower Garden quilts, the pattern being one of the most popular of the era. Dorothy remembered her mother and sisters making the quilts.

By the time Dorothy and Robert embarked on their retirement trip, she was prepared with shoe boxes of cut hexagons. She had always sewn clothing for her daughters, and had scraps from that. Dorothy had also announced her intentions to family and friends who in turn contributed more fabrics.

Eight months and thousands of miles later, Dorothy and Robert returned to Tahoe City. The family teasingly asked Dorothy if she had ever finished that quilt she was going to make and were astounded when she produced not one, but six completed tops!

All of these were traditional versions of the Grandmother's Flower Garden design. It wasn't long before Dorothy began devising original arrangements of the "rosettes" formed by the hexagons. Eventually, she went beyond the traditional and created unique and original designs.

These included intricate mosaic designs as well as figurative patchwork featuring butterflies, baskets, hearts, flags and even roadrunners. By adding small triangles and diamonds, Dorothy created many more hexagon variations of stars, flowers and kaleidoscopes.

Dorothy likes to have several quilts in various stages of completion. "If I can't find the right piece of material, I can put the quilt back and work on something else," she says. She would always take several quilts to work on each summer, when the Wrays returned to the cooler weather of Tahoe.

Dorothy enjoys the planning and making of the quilts more than the quilting process. "While I'm sewing, I'm thinking ahead, trying to decide what color or fabric to use next", she says. "With quilting, there's not much to think about and then I start worrying about all sorts of things!"

Robert contributes too, giving many of the quilts their lovely descriptive titles. More recently, he has been helping even more. After he said he'd like to try hand quilting, Dorothy gave him one of her tops to do (one of her least favorites!). Even though the backing fabric was heavy, Robert did a wonderful job of quilting. He had to make his own thimble, being unable to find one large enough. The Wrays now quilt side by side.

Dorothy has exhibited her quilts, winning lots of ribbons and the admiration of viewers as well. She has been featured as a speaker and guest teacher at quilt shows and has had one-woman shows of her work. At one display of Dorothy's quilts, Robert heard some women making comments, such as, "the colors they used are nice" and "look how they did this one".

Finally, he set them straight. "There's no 'they'," he said, "it's a 'she'!" Dorothy has even received mail addressed simply: "The Hexagon Quilt Lady, Quartzsite, Arizona".

In the spring of 1997, the Wrays sold their Quartzsite home and returned to live year-round in the Sacramento, California, area.

In this volume, Dorothy has gathered her best into a veritable bouquet of quilts. The flowers in bloom may be calico hexagons, yet the colors and beauty of the garden are real. ❧

Look closely at the stars in Desert Grandeur on page 33; they were created by cutting a directional fabric consistently. The fabric had a zigzag design of squares on point. By cutting the hexagons from the same design area, I was able to create the effect of stars in the quilt.

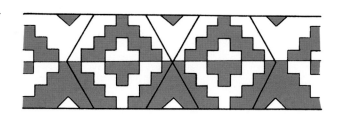

To make centers for some of the rosettes in Desert Grandeur, I cut half-hexagons from the same print. Sewn together they formed a symmetrical design. I made a template for a half hexagon, adding seam allowances.

Triangles and diamonds are used in some of my quilts. For these shapes, I also cut strips first, then cut the triangles and diamonds from these. Use the templates to measure the strips, as described above, or cut strips to the nearest eighth-inch.

Cut 1 1/4 inch strips for the 3/4 inch diamond, 1 3/8 inch strips for the 1 inch diamond, and 2 inch strips for the 1 1/2 inch diamond. The size for the 1 inch diamond is exact; the other sizes include extra that will have to be trimmed.

Cut 1 1/2 inch strips for the 3/4 inch triangle, 1 5/8 inch strips for the 1 inch triangle, and 2 1/4 inch strips for the 1 1/2 inch triangle. The size for the 1 inch triangle is exact; the other sizes include extra that will have to be trimmed.

After the strips are cut, mark the diamonds or triangles by tracing around the templates. Place the diamonds all in one direction. Alternate the direction of the triangle. I always use scissors to cut these shapes because of their small size.

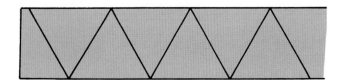

Since some of my designs contain thousands of pieces, you may find that it's best to alternate some cutting with some sewing. Cut enough to get started, then do some sewing for immediate gratification. Only cut as many as you can at one session without getting fatigued and careless.

Sewing

On all of the many quilts I've made, I have simply "eyeballed" the seam allowance. If you are very new to quiltmaking, or find it hard to keep a consistent seam, it would be best to mark a sewing line. Use a ruler to draw a line 1/4 inch from the edges, or make another template without seams and use it to mark the sewing line.

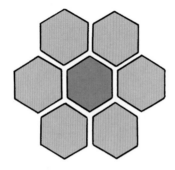

It is most important that the seam allowance be consistent. My seams are actually slightly smaller than 1/4 inch, but they are very uniform. Most antique quilts have seams smaller than 1/4 inch. The stitches on a smaller seam must be extra small for strength. The stitching starts and stops on the sewing line, not the raw edges. The seam allowances must be left free, since the other pieces will be set into them.

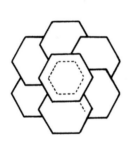

When I sew, I hold the needle steady and move the fabric in an up and down motion with the other hand. I sew the whole side of the hexagon, letting the stitches stack up on the needle, before I pull it through. I just hold the pieces in place instead of pinning.

You'll love the ease and portability of hand sewing these hexagons. Most of my designs are based on the traditional Grandmother's Flower Garden, where concentric rows of hexagons surround a center one, called a rosette. Let me start with that basic unit.

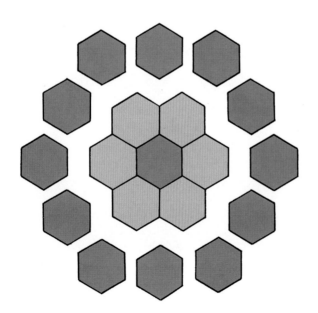

Thread a small betweens needle with a single stand of sewing thread. Remember to always thread the end of the thread as it comes off the spool and knot the other end. This keeps the thread from tangling. Always start and stop each seam on the sewing line. Begin and end each seam with a backstitch.

Arrange a circle of six hexagons around a center one. Sew one of the six to the center. Add the next hexagon to the center, passing the needle through the seam allowances. Continue working in a circle around the center hexagon until all six are added. Sew one side of the last hexagon to the first one. Finish sewing the sides of the hexagons.

Each ring of hexagons is sewn much the same way. The next ring will have twelve hexagons, with every other one having a flat side sewn to a flat side on the first ring. The others will have the pointed side set into the seams of the first ring. Always pass the needle through the seams instead of sewing them down. After the twelve hexagons are added to the first ring, sew the seams between them. Pass through the seams, then pivot the next hexagon so the raw edges align.

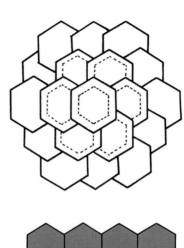

I sew continuous seams whenever possible. I may have an area where I sew just the sides of several hexagons together. I then join the rows with a long continuous seam. You'll soon find that ending and tying off each seam takes more time than the sewing. That's why you'll look for ways to join as many hexagons with one seam as possible.

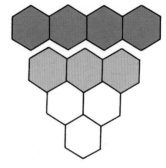

Many of my quilts also use diamonds and triangles. These are also sewn by hand, always 1/4 inch from the seams. They are sewn in the same manner, with the sides of some pieces sewn together and then setting in the other pieces. All of these shapes are based on the hexagon and are either 60° or 120° angles. Some of the triangles are small but the angles are no more difficult than the other pieces.

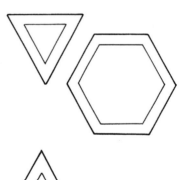

The sewing lines of the hexagons, triangles and diamonds are the same size. The raw edges are not the same size. The tips of the triangles will extend beyond the hexagons. The obtuse angle of the diamond will line up with the angle of the hexagon but the tip will extend beyond. As you sew these shapes, make sure the sewing lines match.

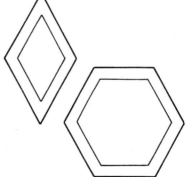

Machine Sewing

My first sixty quilts were all hand sewn. I finally realized that I could use the sewing machine to sew the sides of hexagons together, especially when there were rows and rows of them.

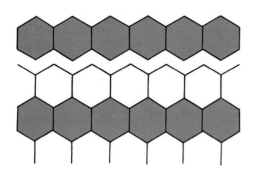

Instead of starting and stopping on the sewing line, which would be very tedious to do, sew from edge to edge. Don't backstitch because you want the seam to open at the ends. You can assembly-line sew several rows at once.

The angled sides of the rows are sewn by hand. The machine seams will pull apart just enough by themselves. Sew the angles, always passing the needles through the seam allowances and beginning and ending each seam with a backstitch.

Assembling

When I first started, I sewed the individual blocks, then joined them together later. When I started creating mosaic and pictorial designs, I began by making the center then working outward until it was the size I wanted. You'll have to find the style of working that suits you best. The beauty of hand piecing is that any shape is possible. Angled seams or set-in seams are just as easy as sewing the hexagons together.

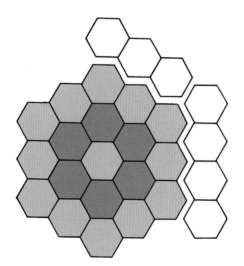

Rosette block

For the traditional Grandmother's Flower Garden quilts, you will want to make all the rosettes first. You could then place them on different colors to see which would be best for the setting hexagons, the "paths" through the garden. You may also change your mind about what arrangement to use.

Several of the other quilts also use a block format. Sometimes the blocks are diamond-shaped, as in Enchanted Horizons (page 32), or have different sizes of blocks, as in the heart and rosette blocks in Love in Bloom (page 29). You'll want to make all the blocks before joining them (a great portable project!) so you can rearrange them before joining them together.

The mosaic designs are best done from the center outward. You may change the design as it grows or change some of the colors. You could even work on the quilt in sections or quarters, and join them later.

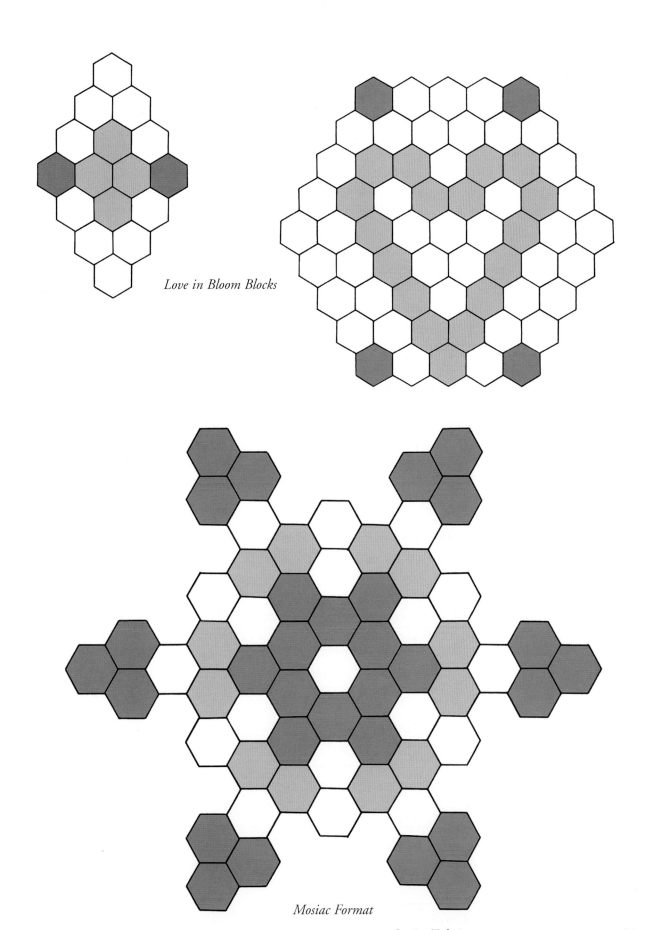

Love in Bloom Blocks

Mosiac Format

QUILT PATTERNS

The patterns presented here include the classic Grandmother's Flower Garden quilt, with both a single path and a triple path. The rest of the patterns are for quilts I have designed or adapted. Feel free to modify them for your own use. Use a larger hexagon for a bigger quilt or just use the center of a pattern for a smaller one. The repeated block patterns are easy to customize; add or subtract rows of blocks for the size you want.

On each pattern, the hexagon size is the finished, or sewn, size. The pattern pieces for templates are on page 65.

All yardage amounts are based on 42 inch wide fabric. They are also based on the method of cutting strips, then cutting hexagons from the strips. In most cases, I have allowed for an extra strip or two. Keep in mind that the smaller the pieces are in the quilt, the more fabric is taken up in seam allowances.

Quilts with centered flowers or figures list only the yardage amounts for an allover print. These fabrics are noted with an asterisk (*). If you choose to center designs, the actual yardage will depend on the repeat of the design in your fabric. Purchase enough fabric to yield the listed number of cut hexagons.

The fabrics for the mosaic variations are listed in the order they appear, from the center outward. The numbers on the quilt drawings refer the steps in making the quilt.

I have referred to the color and print of the fabrics only as a way for you to keep your place in the pattern. I don't expect you to use the colors or prints that I used. Since the fabrics I used in my quilts are long gone, your quilts may be very different from mine. I've always said my quilts are individual, instead of original. Please use my designs to make your own individual quilts!

Grandmother's Flower Garden

Color & Print	Fabric Amount	Cut 1" Hexagon
White	3 3/8 yards	786
Yellow solid	1/2 yard	91
Gold solid	1/4 yard	42
Gold print	1/2 yard	84
4 green solids	1/4 yard each	36 each
4 green prints	1/2 yard each	72 each
4 red solids	1/4 yard each	36 each
4 red prints	1/2 yard each	72 each
5 blue solids	1/4 yard each	36 each
5 blue prints	1/2 yard each	72 each
Medium blue print	1 yard	162
Binding	1 yard	
Backing	5 3/4 yards	

Sewing

1 Make 7 double rosettes using 1 yellow, 6 gold solid and 12 gold print hexagons for each.

2 Make 6 double rosettes from each of the green, red, and blue fabrics using 1 yellow, 6 solid and 12 print hexagons for each. Make a total of 78 blocks.

3 Make 6 partial blocks using 1 yellow, 4 solid and 7 medium blue print hexagons for each.

4 Join the blocks using white hexagons between them. Refer to color picture for placement of the center gold, red and blue blocks.

5 Add the partial blocks to the top and bottom edges. Fill in corners with medium blue print hexagons.

Finishing
Quilt 1/4" from seams. Bind with bias binding.

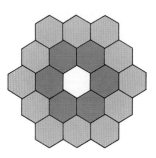

Grandmother's Flower Garden (Triple Path)

Color & Print	Fabric Amount	Cut 1" Hexagon
White solid	3 1/2 yards	828
Yellow solid	1/4 yard	46
12 solids	1/4 yard each	18 each
12 checked	1/3 yard each	36 each
Gold solid	2 3/4 yards	615
Black checked	2 yards	426
Binding	1 yard	
Backing	7 3/4 yards	

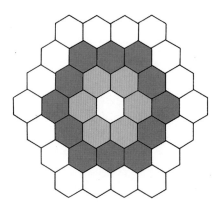

Sewing

1 Make 46 triple rosettes using 1 yellow, 6 solid, 12 checked, and 18 white hexagons for each.

2 Join the blocks with gold hexagons between them.

3 Fill in the scallops on the top and bottom edges using 22 black checked hexagons for each. Add another row of black checked hexagons to those edges.

4 Fill in the side edges with black checked hexagons.

Finishing

Quilt 1/4" from seams. Bind with bias binding.

Grandmother's Flower Garden
by Dorothy Wray, 1976, quilted by Cynthia Thomas. 79"x96.
This is the classic pattern, with two rows of hexagons, one plain and one print, surrounding the center. The rosettes are separated with a single row of white hexagons forming the path through the garden. The fabrics were from my mother's workbasket and date from the 1940's and '50's.

Grandmother's Flower Garden (Triple Path)
by Dorothy Wray, 1973, quilted by Cynthia Thomas. 86"x100". The rosettes are separated by a triple row of hexagons, with white on either side of a color. I used yellow for the path and lots of gingham in the flowers. Many Flower Garden quilts used green for the path.

Pink and Blue Blossoms

Color & Print	Fabric Amount	Cut 1" Hexagon
17 blue prints	1/3 yard each	54 each
Blue/ white print	1/3 yard	50
17 pink prints	1/4 yard each	36 each
Pink/white print	1/2 yard	98
Dark blue print	3/4 yard	150
White print	7/8 yard	168
Blue print	1 1/2 yards	298
Binding	1 yard	
Backing	5 1/2 yards	

Sewing

1 Make 50 double rosettes using 1 blue/white and 18 blue print hexagons for each.

2 Make 98 single rosettes using 1 pink/white and 6 pink print hexagons for each.

3 Join blocks together with dark blue hexagons between them.

4 Add white print and blue print hexagons to the edges of the quilt.

Finishing
Quilt and bind as desired.

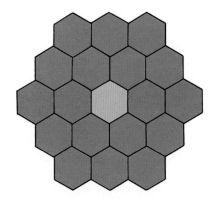

Night Flowers

Color & Print	Fabric Amount	Cut 3/4" Hexagon
Yellow solid	1 yard	288
Black solid	5 1/4 yards	1,716
16 solids	5/8 yard each	144 each*
Binding	1 yard	
Backing	5 1/2 yards	

*Cut 1 additional hexagon of one color and 6 additional of a contrasting color for the center rosette.

Sewing

1 Make 1 rosette using the additional 7 that were cut. Make 12 rosettes using 1 black and 6 yellow hexagons for each. Join to make center star-shaped block.

2 Make 6 blocks using 12 yellow, 12 black, and 37 solid color hexagons for each. Join to center star, adding black hexagons.

3 Make 38 blocks using 1 yellow, 12 black, 12 of one color and 36 contrasting color hexagons for each. (Each color should be used for the center rosette on 3 blocks and for the outer rosettes on 3 other blocks.)

4 Make 98 rosettes using 1 yellow and 6 black hexagons for each.

5 Make 8 partial blocks using 1 yellow, 4 black, 6 of one color and 18 contrasting color hexagons for each.

6 Join the blocks, alternating the large blocks with the black rosettes and filling in with black hexagons.

7 Add the partial blocks to the top and bottom edges. Add black hexagons to the edges.

Finishing
Quilt as desired. Bind with bias binding.

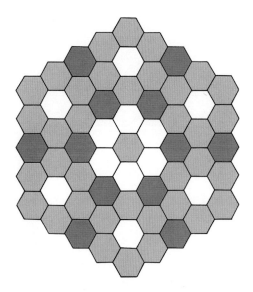

Pink and Blue Blossoms *by Dorothy Wray, 1987. 71"x92". Larger blue flowers alternate with smaller pink ones, with single dark hexagons placed between the flowers.*

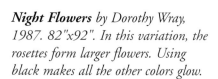

Night Flowers *by Dorothy Wray, 1987. 82"x92". In this variation, the rosettes form larger flowers. Using black makes all the other colors glow.*

Paisley Waltz

Color & Print	Fabric Amount	Cut 1 1/2" Hexagon
Purple solid	3/4 yard	64
Yellow paisley	1 1/3 yards*	136
Lavender print	1/4 yard*	20
Green print	3/8 yard*	28
Peach paisley	1/2 yard*	36
White paisley	2 yards*	216
Lavender solid	3/4 yard	60
Green solid	3/4 yard	62
Peach solid	3/4 yard	62
Dark green print	1/2 yard	36
Dark peach solid	3/8 yard	28
Dark green solid	2 1/4 yards	224
Binding	1 yard	
Backing	5 yards	

Amounts are for an allover print. To center a printed design, purchase enough fabric to yield the correct number of cut hexagons.

Sewing

1 Working from the center outward, join rows of hexagons into a large diamond shape.

2   Continue adding rows of hexagons to the sides of the large diamond shape.

2 Add dark green solid hexagons to edges of quilt. Add a row of white paisley hexagons and finish with another row of dark green hexagons.

Finshing

Quilt 1/4" from seams. Bind with narrow binding or use the facing method. For facing method, cut 132 dark green solid hexagons from 1 1/4 yard of fabric. Sew and attach as described in the text.

Paisley Waltz *by Dorothy Wray, 1991. 69"x84".*

Enchanted Roses

Color & Print	Fabric Amount	Cut 1" Hexagon	Cut 1" Diamond
White	4 7/8 yards	1,186	16
Red solid	2 3/8 yards	537	8
Rose print on dark	2 yards*	444	
Rose print on light	5/8 yard*	132	
Leaf print	5/8 yard*	132	
Butterfly print	3/8 yard*	66	
Binding	1 yard		
Backing	6 1/4 yards		

*Amounts are for an allover print. To center a printed design, purchase enough fabric to yield the correct number of cut hexagons.

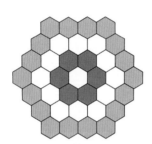

Sewing

1 Make 11 triple rosettes using 1 red center, 6 dark roses, 12 light roses, 12 leaf print and 6 butterfly prints for each. Surround with 18 white hexagons each.

2 Make 52 single rosettes using 1 red center and 6 dark roses for each.

3 Make 4 large triangle blocks using 1 dark rose and 29 white hexagons for each.

4 Make 12 small triangle blocks using 6 white hexagons for each.

5 Make 4 bow blocks using 23 red and 8 white hexagons for each. Sew diamonds into hexagons for bow ends using 1 red and 2 white diamonds for each.

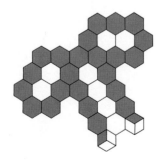

6 Join the blocks using red hexagons between them. Following the picture, fill in with remaining white and dark rose hexagons. Work outward from the center. Form borders with dark rose print and red hexagons.

Finishing
Quilt 1/4 inch from seams. I used the facing technique to bind the quilt. Cut an additional 226 red hexagons and sew into the same formation as the quilt edges. Attach as described in the text.

Victorian Rose Garden

Color & Print	Fabric Amount	Cut 1" Hexagon
White	2 yards	460
Green print	3 yards	682
Pink rose print	1/2 yard*	80
Aqua rose print	1/4 yard*	36
Leaf print	7/8 yard*	189
Pink/green leaf	5/8 yard*	120
Pink bud print	1/2 yard*	112
24 flower prints	1/8 yard*	7 each
Butterfly print	1/4 yard*	26
Bug print	1/8 yard*	8
Binding	1 yard	
Backing	4 3/4 yards	

Amounts are for an allover print. To center a printed design, purchase enough fabric to yield the correct number of cut hexagons.

Sewing

1 Make 1 double rosette using 13 leaf and 6 pink rose print hexagons.

2 Make 6 oblong blocks using 1 butterfly, 8 white (or 6 white and 2 bug print), 14 leaf, 24 assorted flower prints, and either 28 pink/green leaf or 28 pink bud print hexagons for each.

3 Make 6 blocks using 1 pink rose, 6 aqua rose, and 7 pink/green leaf print for each. Join to center rosette and large oblong blocks, filling in with green print and pink rose print hexagons.

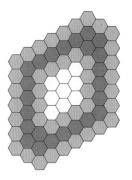

4 Make 16 blocks using 1 flower and 2 green print hexagons for each. Join with butterfly print and white hexagons to make corner sections.

5 Join pink rose, leaf print, green print and pink/green leaf print hexagons to the top and bottom edges.

6 Join pink rose, green print and leaf print hexagons to the side edges.

Finishing

Quilt 1/4 inch from seams. Bind with narrow binding or use the facing method. For facing method, cut an additional 194 green print hexagons. Sew into the same formation as the quilt edges and attach as described in the text.

Enchanted Roses *by Dorothy Wray, 1992, quilted by Ada Russell. 83"x106". Scarlet ribbons weave between the bouquets and make pretty bows. A printed rose forms the bouquets and accents the background and border.*

Victorian Rose Garden *by Dorothy Wray, 1987. 70"x78". By centering leaves as well as flowers, the bouquets in this quilts have a soft, watercolor look. A green print in the background adds texture and color.*

Love in Bloom, *pieced by Dorothy Wray, 1994, quilted by Ada Russell. 71"x92".*
These hearts are blooming with lots of multi-colored roses. The design would also work
with other types of prints in pretty colors.

Love in Bloom

Color & Print	Fabric Amount	Cut 3/4" Hexagon
White	4 1/4 yards	1,360
White eyelet print	7/8 yard	245
35 various prints	1/8 yard each*	17 each
Rose print on light	3/8 yard*	96
Green print	1 1/8 yards	312
Rose print on dark	1 1/8 yards*	336
Pink print	2 yards	624
Bow print	1/4 yard*	35
Binding	1 yard	
Backing	5 3/8 yards	

Amounts are for an allover print. To center a printed design, purchase enough fabric to yield the correct number of cut hexagons.

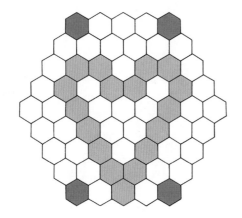

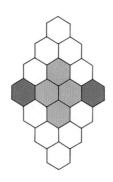

Sewing

1 Make 35 heart blocks, using 1 bow print, 7 eyelet print, 17 print, 4 green and 32 white hexagons for each.

2 Make 24 diamond blocks, using 4 light rose, 2 green and 10 white hexagons for each.

3 Join the blocks using pink, green and dark rose print hexagons between them.

4 Border quilt with pink and dark rose print hexagons.

Finishing

Quilt 1/4 inch from seams. Bind with narrow bias binding.

Enchanted Horizons

Color & Print	Fabric Amount	Cut 1" Hexagon
White/blue & dark navy	5/8 yard each	120 each
Pale blue & medium navy	5/8 yard each	120 each
Light blue & dark royal	3/4 yard each	156 each
Gray/blue & medium royal	1 yard each	198
Medium blue	7/8 yard	192
Pale pink & dark burgundy	1/2 yard each	95 each
Light pink & burgundy	1/2 yard each	95 each
Light rose & dark wine	5/8 yard each	124 each
Medium rose & wine	3/4 yard each	157 each
Medium pink	7/8 yard	186
Binding	1 yard	
Backing	5 1/2 yards	

Sewing

1 Make 30 blue diamond blocks and 29 pink diamond blocks. For each, use the following number of hexagons (from lightest to darkest): 3, 3, 4, 5, 6, 5, 4, 3, 3.

2 Make 4 blue half-diamond blocks and 4 pink half-diamond blocks. For each, use the following number of hexagons (from lightest to darkest): 2, 2, 2, 3, 3, 3, 2, 2, 2.

3 Make 12 blue triangle blocks. For each, use the following number of hexagons (6 from dark to medium and 6 from light to medium): 3, 3, 4, 5.

4 Make 4 blue corner blocks. For each, use the following number of hexagons (2 from dark to medium and 2 from light to medium): 2, 2, 2, 3.

5 Join blocks in concentric diamonds by color. Fill in with partial blocks.

Finishing

Quilt 1/4 inch from the seams and form diamonds within each block. Bind as desired. I used a pretty printed stripe, cutting the binding strip twice as wide as the stripe plus seams.

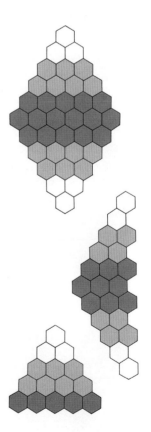

Enchanted Horizons *by Dorothy Wray, 1988, quilted by Lucille Haines. 75"x93".*
Hexagons form shaded diamonds using nine fabrics each in blues and pinks.
The diamonds are then arranged into a larger diamond design.

Desert Grandeur, *pieces by Dorothy Wray, 1992, quilted by Robert and Dorothy Wray, 1993. 70"x75". Inspired by the beautiful colors of the Arizona desert, this quilt has several Southwest-style prints. One print formed stars when the hexagons were joined.*

Desert Grandeur

Color & Print	Fabric Amount	Cut 3/4" Hexagon
Cream print	3 1/4 yards	1,000
Peach print	3 1/2 yards	1,077
Aqua dotted	1 yard	232
Green cactus print	1 yard*	234
Peach cactus print	3/8 yard*	84
Zigzag print	2 1/4 yards*	634
Binding	1 yard	
Backing	4 1/2 yards	

Amounts are for an allover print. To center a printed design, purchase enough fabric to yield the correct number of cut hexagons.

Sewing

1 Make 1 double rosette using 1 pieced center, 6 zigzag print and 12 cream hexagons.

2 Make 6 overlapping rosettes using 2 pieced centers, 6 print, 4 contrasting print and 9 cream hexagons for each.

3 Make 12 rosettes using 1 pieced center and 6 print hexagons for each.

4 Join together, filling in with peach print and green cactus print hexagons. Surround center with rows of cream and peach cactus print hexagons.

5 Make diamond blocks using aqua dotted, peach print and green cactus print hexagons.

6 Make 72 rosettes using peach or pieced centers and 6 print hexagons for each. Make 12 partial rosettes using 1 peach and 4 print hexagons for each. Fill in with cream, peach cactus, zigzag, peach print, and aqua dotted hexagons.

7 Fill in the edges with cream print and peach print hexagons.

Finishing
Quilt 1/4 inch from seams. Bind with straight strips cut 2 inches wide.

Birth of the Blue Rose

Color & Print	Fabric Amount	Cut 1" Hexagon
Pink bow	7/8 yard*	169
Light blue rose	1/8 yard*	12
Navy leaf	5/8 yard	108
Blue rose/leaf	1/4 yard*	18
Blue/pink print	1 1/8 yards*	228
Small blue roses	1/3 yard	54
Butterfly	1/3 yard*	56
Blue bow	1/8 yard*	16
Rosebud print	3 1/4 yard	730
Navy solid	2 7/8 yards	650
Blue rose	3/4 yard*	126
Border stripe	2 1/2 yards	2 at 3" x 78"
		2 at 3" x 85"
Binding	1 yard	
Backing	5 yards	

Amounts are for an allover print. To center a printed design, purchase enough fabric to yield the correct number of cut hexagons.

Sewing

1 Make 1 triple rosette using 1 pink bow, 12 light blue rose, 12 navy leaf, and 12 butterfly print hexagons.

2 Make 6 diamond blocks using 9 blue/pink print for each. Make 6 blocks using 1 pink bow and 3 blue rose/leaf print hexagons for each. Join to center, filling in with navy leaf, butterfly, and pink bow hexagons.

3 Make 18 triangle blocks using 6 rosebud print hexagons for each. Make 12 diamond blocks using 1 butterfly, 3 small blue rose print, and 12 navy hexagons for each.

4 Make 6 rosettes using 1 pink bow, 3 small blue rose and 3 blue butterfly print hexagons for each. Join to center, filling in with rosebud, butterfly and navy hexagons.

5 Surround center with rows of pink bow, blue/pink print and navy hexagons.

6 Make blocks for the corner areas using 4 blue bow and 15 blue/pink print hexagons for each. Fill in with rosebud and blue butterfly print hexagons.

7 Make 26 diamond blocks using 1 pink bow and 3 blue rose print hexagons for each. Filling in with rosebud print and navy solid hexagons, join to the top and bottom edges.

8 Make 16 partial rosettes using 1 pink bow, 3 blue rose, and 2 navy solid hexagons for each. Filling in with rosebud print and navy, join to the side edges.

Finishing
Edge with a border stripe. Quilt 1/4 inch from seams. Bind as desired.

Birth of the Blue Rose by Dorothy Wray, 1993. 78"x82". This quilt celebrates the development of the world's first blue rose. Scientists were able to clone a blue gene from the petunia.

Purple Haze, *pieced by Dorothy Wray, 1986, quilted by Robert and Dorothy Wray, 1992. 80"x84". Purple and peach complement beautifully in this mosaic quilt. The green roses and butterflies were cut from the same fabric.*

Purple Haze

Color & Print	Fabric Amount	Cut 3/4" Hexagon
Purple rose print	1/2 yards*	115
Peach rose print	1/4 yard*	30
Purple solid	3 3/4 yards	1194
Pink rose on white	1 3/4 yards*	484
Dark peach pansy print	1/8 yard*	18
Medium peach print	1/3 yard	72
Green rose print	3/8 yard*	90
Green butterfly print	7/8 yard*	240
Pale lavender print	1/8 yard	12
Lavender solid	7/8 yard	252
Peach/lavender print	1 1/4 yards	324
Light peach print	3/4 yard	160
Medium lavender print	2 1/4 yards	628
Peach rose/blue leaf	1/2 yard*	118
Purple print	1/4 yard	48
Lavender solid	2 1/2 yards	2 at 4"x70" 2 at 8"x87"
Binding	1 yard	
Backing	5 1/4 yards	

Amounts are for an allover print. To center a printed design, purchase enough fabric to yield the correct number of cut hexagons.

Sewing

1 Make 1 rosette using 1 purple rose and 6 peach rose print hexagons. Make 6 rosettes using 1 peach rose and 6 purple rose print hexagons for each. Join, adding 6 purple rose print hexagons, to make the center.

2 Make 18 rosettes, using 1 peach rose and 6 pink rose on white hexagons for each. Following the diagram, fill in with additional purple rose print, purple solid, peach pansy, and peach print hexagons. Join to center.

3 Make 42 rosettes using 1 medium lavender and 6 peach/lavender print hexagons for each. Fill in with lavender and purple solid, pale lavender, green butterfly and light peach print hexagons.

4 Make 12 double rosettes using 7 peach rose/blue leaf and 12 pink on white print hexagons for each. Fill in with lavender solid, green butterfly and purple rose print hexagons.

5 Make 4 star-shaped units for the corners using 7 peach rose/blue leaf, 12 purple print, 18 green butterfly print and 30 pink rose on white hexagons for each.

6 Make 16 rosettes using 7 pink rose on white hexagons for each. Make 12 rosettes using 1 lavender and 6 peach and lavender print hexagons for each. Fill in with lavender print and purple solid hexagons. Join to star-shaped units to form outer edges of the quilt.

7 Applique the top and bottom edges to two border pieces. Repeat for side borders. Sew the corner seams then trim the excess fabric from behind the hexagons.

Finishing
Quilt 1/4 inch from the seams. Bind with straight strips cut 2 inches wide.

Secret Garden, *pieced by Dorothy Wray, 1993, quilted by Robert and Dorothy Wray, 1995. 70"x77". After seeing the film, The Secret Garden, with my granddaughter, Natalie Quinn, I knew I had to make a quilt showing the beautiful colors and flowers of a garden. The gray print was perfect for the paths through a formal English garden.*

Secret Garden

Color & Print	Fabric Amount	Cut 3/4" Hexagon
Red spray	1/8 yard*	7
Small red print	1/4 yard*	28
Red rose print	1/4 yard*	42
Green leaf/dark	1 1/4 yards	326
Gray rock print	3 1/2 yards	1,106
Peach tulip	1/4 yard*	40
Pansy print	1/4 yard*	24
Lavender roses	1/4 yard*	24
Pink roses	1/4 yard*	44
Red/black print	1/8 yard*	16
Blue flowers	1/4 yard*	32
Goose print	1/8 yard*	12
Bunny print	1/8 yard*	12
Bird print	1/4 yard*	44
Green rose	1/2 yard*	118
18 flower prints	1/4 yard each*	47 each
10 leaf prints	1/4 yard each*	41 each
Bright flowers	1/3 yard*	60
Gray solid	1/8 yard	12
Pink/black print	1/4 yard	32
Butterfly print	1/4 yard*	34
Binding	1 yard	
Backing	4 3/4 yards	

*Amounts allow for an allover print. To center a printed design, purchase enough fabric to yield the correct number of cut hexagons.

Sewing

1 Make 1 triple rosette using 7 red spray, 12 small red flower, and 18 red rose print hexagons. Surround with small leaf and rock print hexagons.

2 Make 6 blocks using 6 peach tulip hexagons for each. Make 4 blocks using 6 pansy print hexagons for each. Join to center, adding rock print hexagons.

3 Make 4 oblong blocks using 4 lavender rose, 5 pink rose, and 17 small leaf print hexagons for each. Join to center section, adding rock print hexagons between the sections.

4 Fill in top and bottom of center with red rose, red/black, and rock print hexagons.

5 Make 20 rosettes using 7 hexagons of the same floral print for each. Make 4 partial rosettes using 5 hexagons of the same floral print for each. Make 22 groups using 3 hexagons of the same floral print for each. Adding small leaf, butterfly and rock print hexagons, join to top and bottom of center section.

6 Make 4 wedge-shaped sections using 16 small leaf, 8 blue flower, 2 lavender rose, 6 pink rose, 13 green rose, and 3 duck print hexagons for each.

7 Make 30 rosettes using 7 hexagons of the same floral print for each. Make 4 partial rosettes using 6 hexagons of the same floral for each. Make 22 groups using 3 of the same floral print for each. Make 4 groups using 3 green leaf print for each. Add small leaf, butterfly, and rock print hexagons. Join to sides of center section, adding wedge-shaped sections from previous step.

8 Make 18 rosettes using 7 hexagons of the same floral print for each. Make 4 partial rosettes using 6 hexagons of the same floral print for each. Adding small leaf and rock print hexagons, add to top and bottom of center section.

9 Make 24 rosettes using 7 hexagons of the same floral print for each. Adding leaf and rock print hexagons, add to sides of center section. Fill in corners using gray solid, pink/black, bird, small leaf and rock print hexagons.

10 Make 42 groups using 4 hexagons of the same leaf print for each. Adding bright floral and bird print hexagons, join to top and bottom edges.

11 Make 42 groups using 5 hexagons of the same leaf print for each. Make 4 groups using 4 hexagons of the same leaf print for each. Adding bright floral, bird and rock print hexagons, join to side edges.

12 Fill in outer edges with rock print hexagons, adding bright floral print in the corners.

Finishing
Quilt 1/4 inch from the seams. Bind with straight strips cut 2 inches wide.

Kansas Sunflowers

Color & Print	Fabric Amount	Cut 1 1/2" Hexagon	Cut 1 1/2" Diamond
Brown print	1/2 yard	36	
Yellow dot	5/8 yard		144
Gold print	1 1/8 yards		360
Green print	1 1/2 yards		429
Yellow checked	7 5/8 yards	582	420
Solid green	3 yards	Cut 2 at 5" x 75"	
		Cut 2 at 5" x 98"	
Binding	1 yard		
Backing	5 1/2 yards		

Sewing

1 Make 22 blocks using 1 brown print, 6 checked hexagons and 6 yellow, 12 gold, 12 green and 6 checked diamonds for each. Make 2 blocks using 1 brown print and 4 checked hexagons and 6 yellow, 12 gold, 10 green and 5 checked diamonds for each.

3 Make 12 blocks using 1 brown print hexagon and 6 gold and 12 checked diamonds for each. Note: These blocks are directional.

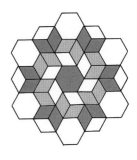

4 Make 52 double-leaf blocks using 1 checked and 2 green diamonds for each. Make 40 single-leaf blocks using 1 green and 2 checked diamonds for each.

6 Join 4 large blocks, using the 2 with fewer green diamonds. Fill in with checked hexagons and checked and green diamonds to make center section. Add 28 double-leaf blocks to the center section. Add the small blocks to the top and bottom of the center section.

9 Add 8 large blocks to the top and bottom of the center section. Fill in with checked hexagons and double-leaf blocks. Add 12 large blocks to the sides of the center section. Fill in with checked hexagons and single-leaf blocks.

11 Applique the side edges to the border pieces. Sew straight borders to the top and bottom edges. Sew corners and trim the excess.

Finishing
Quilt next to the diamonds. Quilt the diamond formation on the hexagons. Bind as desired.

Kansas Sunflowers, pieced by Dorothy Wray, 1983, quilted by Violet Mattice. 72"x94". These big, bright flowers remind me of my native state. The background is made of hexagons, quilted to echo the diamonds in the blocks.

Meadow Flowers by Dorothy Wray, 1988. 67"x89". A green meadow filled with wildflowers - each one with centered flowers. This quilt is perfect for using those smaller cuts of fabric in your collection that have nice flowers.

Meadow Flowers

Color & Print	Fabric Amount	Cut 1" Hexagon	Cut 1" Diamond
Light green print	3 yards	690	
Medium green print	3 1/4 yards	204	1,218
24 flower prints	1/4 yard each*	24 each	
Binding	1 yard		
Backing	5 1/4 yards		

Amounts are for an allover print. To center a printed design, purchase enough fabric to yield the correct number of cut hexagons.

Sewing

1 Make 95 blocks, using 12 medium green diamonds and 6 flower print hexagons for each.

2 Make 230 triangle blocks using 3 light green print hexagons for each.

3 Join flower blocks to triangle blocks.

4 Form a border using medium green hexagons and diamonds.

Finishing
Quilt and bind as desired. For facing technique, cut an additional 204 medium green print hexagons. Sew into the same formation as the quilt edges. Attach as described in the text.

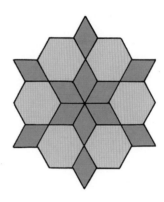

Flower Baskets

Color & Print	Fabric Amount	Cut 3/4" Hexagon	Cut 3/4" Diamond/Triangle	
White	7 1/2 yards	2,526	24	
20 assorted solids	1/4 yard each	28 each		
20 assorted prints	1/4 yard each	42 each		
Yellow dot	5/8 yard	139		
Green dot	2 1/2 yards	398	726	104
Binding	1 yard			
Backing	7 3/4 yards			

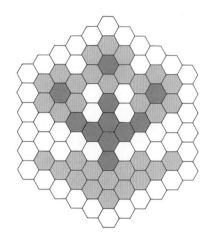

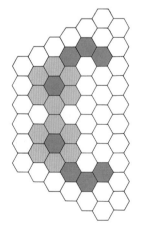

Sewing

1 Make 39 blocks using 14 solid, 6 each of 3 prints, 3 yellow, 8 green, and 48 white hexagons for each.

2 Make 12 rosettes using 1 yellow and 6 print. Fill in with 41white and 6 green hexagons to make 6 partial blocks for the sides.

3 Set the full and partial blocks together with green diamonds and triangles. Fill in the sides with green diamonds and white hexagons.

4 Make 10 rosettes using 1 yellow, 6 print and 4 green hexagons for each. Fill in with white hexagons and diamonds for the top and bottom edges.

Finishing

Quilt 1/4 inch from seams. Bind with straight strips, cut 2 1/2 inches wide.

Butterflies

Color & Print	Fabric Amount	Cut 1" Hexagon	Cut 1" Diamonds/Triangles	
Tan print	4 1/2 yards	1,065		
Brown dot	1 5/8 yards	135	418	63
21 dark prints	1/4 yard each	24 each		
6 dark prints	1/8 yard each	12 each		
21 light prints	1/8 yard each	6 each		
6 light prints	1/8 yard each	3 each		
Binding	1 yard			
Backing	5 1/4 yards			

Sewing

1 Make 21 butterfly blocks using 5 brown dot, 6 light, 24 dark, and 45 tan print hexagons for each.

2 Make 6 partial blocks using 5 brown dot, 3 light, 12 dark, and 20 tan print hexagons for each. Sew diamonds into 30 hexagons using 1 brown and 2 tan for each. Use 5 pieced hexagons for each partial block.

3 Cut solid brown bias tape into 4 inch lengths to make antenna. Applique in place.

4 Join blocks with brown dot diamonds and triangles. Add brown dot diamonds to the edges of the quilt.

Finishing

Quilt 1/4 inch from seams. Bind with straight strips cut 2 inches wide.

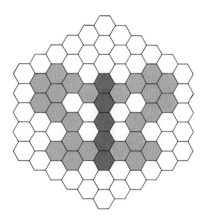

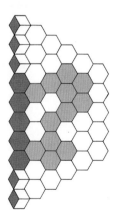

Flower Baskets *by Dorothy Wray, 1979, quilted by Saundra Dee Davis, 1984. 87"x95". This is a great opportunity to use up lots of scraps. Let every flower be a different print.*

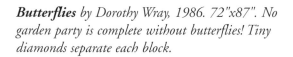

Butterflies *by Dorothy Wray, 1986. 72"x87". No garden party is complete without butterflies! Tiny diamonds separate each block.*

Snow Flowers

Snow Flowers by Dorothy Wray, 1989. 69"x89".
*Diamonds, triangles and hexagons are used to make this
quilt, which is named for the small flowers which bloom
in the Sierras just as the last snow is melting. Pink at first,
the petals gradually darken to a brilliant red.*

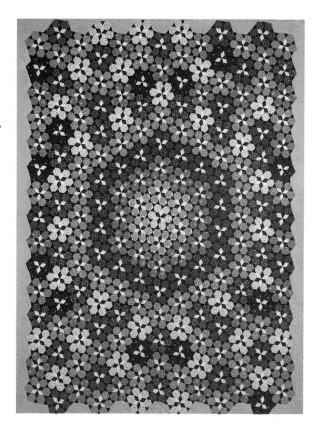

Color & Print	Fabric Amount	Cut 1" Hexagon	Cut 1" Diamond/Triangle	
White dotted	1 1/4 yards		603	
Navy dotted	3 1/4 yards		603	1,606
Pink/white print	1 yard	204		
Pink rose print	1/4 yard*	36		
Medium pink print	1 1/8 yards	240		
Red print	1 yard	222		
Small pink print	1 1/3 yards	282		
Medium red print	3/4 yard	120		
Wine print	1/2 yard	78		
Mauve print	1/4 yard	24		
Pink solid	2 1/2 yards	Cut 2 at 6"x72" Cut 2 at 6"x84"		
Binding	1 yard			
Backing	5 1/4 yards			

*Amounts are for an allover print. To center a printed design, purchase
enough fabric to yield the correct number of cut hexagons.*

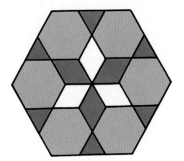

Sewing

1 Sew 3 white and 3 navy dotted diamonds to form a star. Add 6 hexagons and 6 navy triangles to make each block. For a total of 201 blocks, make 34 with the pink/white print, 6 with the pink rose print, 40 with the medium pink print, 37 with the red print, 47 with the bright pink print, 20 with the medium red, 13 with the dark red print and 4 with the mauve print.

2 Join the blocks, adding navy triangles between them. Form 4 rings of color in the center as shown in the quilt. Arrange and join the remaining blocks.

3 Applique the sides to the side border pieces. Applique the top and bottom edges. Sew the corner seams then trim the excess border fabric from behind the hexagons.

Finishing

Quilt 1/4 inch from seams on just the hexagons. Quilt a swirl or other design in the solid borders. Bind as desired. I brought the front to the back and hand stitched in place.

Joann's Dream Garden

Color & Print	Fabric Amount	Cut 3/4" Hexagon
Blue solid	3/4 yard	186
White solid	1/3 yard	67
Rock print	1/4 yard	26
Fern leaf	1/4 yard	26
Pansy print	3/8 yard*	90
Ivy leaf	1/4 yard	24
4 leaf prints	1/8 yard each*	3 to 10 each
7 flower prints	1/8 yard each*	6 to 16 each
Navy print	3/4 yard	174
Accent pieces (birds, clouds,flowers, trees) to applique		
Binding	1/2 yard	
Backing	1 1/4 yards	

Amounts are for an allover print. To center a printed design, purchase enough fabric to yield the correct number of cut hexagons.

Sewing

1 Sew 48 white to flower and leaf print hexagons to form fence.

2 Sew 19 white to 6 blue, 12 flower print and 6 rock print hexagons to form arch. Add flower and leaf print hexagons to arch.

3 Following the picture or your own design, arrange the flower and leaf hexagons for the area above the fence. Join the fence and arch sections. Join blue hexagons to form sky.

4 Arrange pansy, rock print, ivy leaf and other flower and leaf print hexagons to form foreground. Join and add to fence section.

5 Add a double row of navy print hexagons to outside edges.

6 Fuse or applique accent pieces, such as trees, leaves, birds, clouds and large flowers cut from various prints.

Finishing

Quilt 1/4" from seams. Bind as desired.

***Joann's Dream Garden** by Dorothy Wray, 1996. 30"x34". For my daughter, Joann McKeeman, I created a garden where the flowers bloom in profusion and will never fade away. The clouds, trees, and little birds are applique accents. (Shown on back cover.)*

Rosemary's Old English Garden *by Dorothy Wray, 1996. 35"x31". Made for my daughter, Rosemary Quinn. I centered printed roses, daisies, sunflowers and more to give this garden its realistic look. As an accent, I added some applique flowers.*

Rosemary's Old English Garden

Color & Print	Fabric Amount	Cut 3/4" Hexagon	Cut 3/4" Diamond
Blue swirl	1/2 yard	99	
Fern leaf	1/3 yard	72	
Dark green	1/4 yard	31	
Brown	1/8 yard	4	
Gold solid	1/4 yard		22
Gold print	1/4 yard		44
Daisy print	1/4 yard*	28	
4 leaf prints	1/8 yard each*	9 to 15 each	
17 flower prints	1/8 yard each*	5 to 15 each	
Various purples	1/8 yard each	2 to 10 each	
Black solid	5/8 yard	168	
Rose/black print	1/4 yard*	42	
Leaf/black print	1/4 yard*	42	
Large flowers to applique			
Binding	1/2 yard		
Backing	1 1/4 yards		

Amounts are for an allover print. To center a printed design, purchase enough fabric to yield the correct number of cut hexagons.

Sewing

1 Make 3 sunflower blocks using 1 brown hexagon, 6 gold solid and 12 gold print diamonds for each.

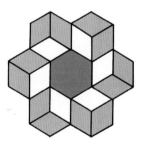

2 Make 1 sunflower block with 1 brown hexagon, 4 gold solid and 8 gold print diamonds for each.

3 Following the picture or your own design, arrange the flowers in clusters. Join in rows or sections.

4 Add black hexagons to the edges. Add a row of alternating rose and leaf print hexagons. Add a final row of black hexagons.

5 Fuse or applique large flowers and stems as an accent.

Finishing
Quilt 1/4" from seams. Bind with narrow binding. Applique the flowers.

FINISHING TECHNIQUES

Hexagons quilts, because of the shape of the basic unit, pose some challenges when it's time to finish them. Without any right-angles, they cannot be bordered and bound like other quilts. I've developed several different methods for adding borders and bindings.

Borders

Several of my quilts have "built-in" borders, rows of contrasting colored hexagons that frame the design. These are sewn by hand in the same manner that the quilt was made. I think that final border of red hexagons in Enchanted Roses (page 28) adds just the right finishing touch.

On some of my quilts, I add more hexagons in a different fabric to fill in the scalloped edges. For instance, on my Triple Path Grandmother's Flower Garden (page 21), I filled in the edges with a black and white check. This framed the scallops and created an even edge for binding.

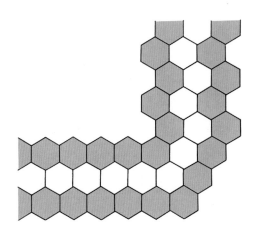

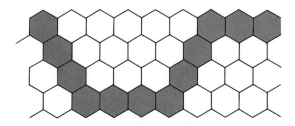

To make the quilt larger, to frame it, or to straighten the edges, you may decide to add straight borders. These add an interesting dimension to the quilt, especially if several different colors are used. I usually do this if the quilt design results in deep scallops on the edges.

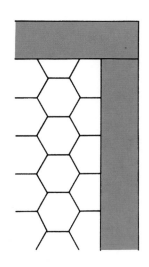

There are two types of straight-edge borders. In the first, the hexagons are cut off by the border. However, first sew the border strips to the quilt top. The angled edges of the hexagons are cut away. This prevents the edges from stretching.

In the second type, the scalloped effect is combined with a straight border. Cut the border wider than the finished size and place it beneath the scalloped edges of the quilt top. Turn under the seams of the outside hexagons and applique the edges to the border piece. After the applique is completed, cut away the excess border from behind.

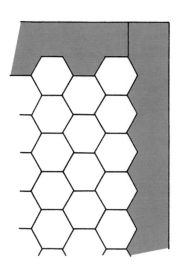

The quilts that have straight borders have those amounts and sizes listed in the quilt directions. The measurements include extra in both the width and length, in case your quilt finishes slightly larger.

Basting

After the quilt top is assembled, press it carefully. If you are planning to quilt away from the seams, the seam allowances don't have to face in any particular direction. If you are planning to quilt in the seam line, or "in the ditch", press the seams accordingly.

The large quilts require more than one length of fabric for the back. Always allow two or three inches excess fabric on all sides. Sew the lengths together, then press the seams open. For the largest quilts, three widths are required since two lengths are not wide enough.

Prepare your top for quilting by layering the backing, batting and top together. Some large frames do not require any basting. If you are using a smaller frame or hoop, the layers should be carefully basted together first.

Spread the backing on the floor or a table (put the width of the quilt across the length of the table). Spread the batting on top. Fold the quilt top in quarters with the wrong side showing. Place it on the batting and unfold it. Make sure the top is centered on the other layers.

Using a long needle and a single strand of thread, baste the layers together with large running stitches. Baste in a grid about every six inches. Baste the outside edges with a smaller stitch. Don't trim the excess batting and backing yet. It will be easier to quilt the outside edges of the quilt with those layers in the frame or hoop.

Quilting

The traditional way to quilt the Grandmother's Flower Garden pattern is 1/4 inch from the seams in every hexagon. This may sound like a lot of quilting, but looks the best on the larger hexagons. The quilting can also echo the shape of the rosette. On my pictorial and mosaic designs, I quilt around the pattern of the quilt. This highlights a certain area or motif.

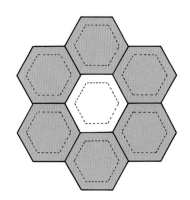

Whether you are quilting along the seam line or 1/4 inch away from the seams, there is no need to mark. Simply "eyeball" the sewing line. Decorative quilting in plain areas or borders can be marked first using a chalk pencil.

You can use a neutral color of thread for the whole quilt or use different colors for different areas. I like to use gray thread on dark colors (even on black), and white on everything else.

Thread a small betweens needle with quilting thread and tie a knot in the end. Begin and end each line of stitching by popping the knot through the top into the batting. Make your stitches nice and even; small stitches will come with practice.

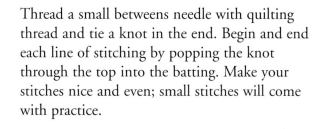

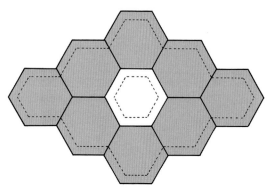

If the quilt is rolled on a frame, you will be quilting from one edge to the other. If you are using a hoop or small frame, start in the middle and work toward the edges.

My husband Robert has devised a system for continuous quilting. It involves passing the needle through the batting from one hexagon to the next, saving time and thread.

When the quilt has the points of the hexagons in a vertical position, it is quilted in horizontal rows. Referring to the diagram, quilt four sides of the hexagon. Pass the needle between the quilt top and back, bringing it out on the side of the next hexagon. Quilt four sides as before. Continue quilting the lower four sides of the row of hexagons.

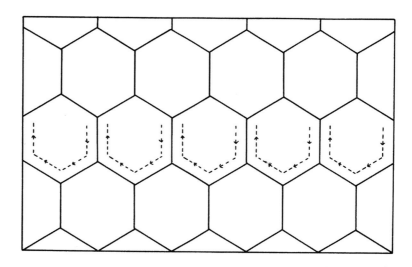

To complete the row, return to the starting place. Quilt the top two sides of each hexagon, passing the needle through the layers to the next hexagon in the row. Right-handed people will work from right to left; left-handed people will work left to right.

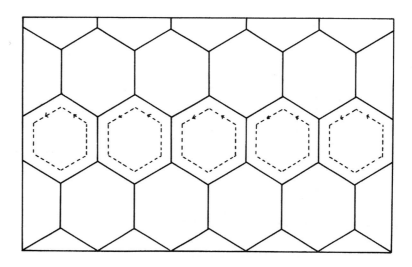

When the quilt has the points of the hexagons in a horizontal position, it is quilted in diagonal rows. Referring to the diagram, quilt four sides of the hexagon. Pass the needle between the quilt top and back, bringing it out on the point of the next hexagon on the diagonal. Quilt four sides as before. Continue quilting four sides of each hexagon, working upward in a diagonal row.

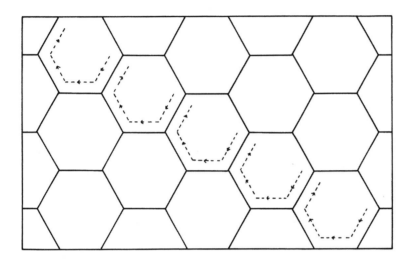

To complete the row, return to the starting place. Quilt the remaining two sides of each hexagon, passing the needle through the layers to the next hexagon in the diagonal row. Right-handed people will begin in the lower right-hand corner and work upward to the left in a diagonal row. Left-handed people will begin in the lower left-hand corner and work upward to the right in a diagonal row.

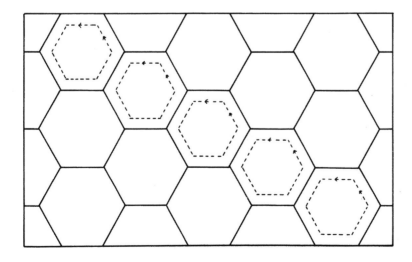

Binding

I use several different methods to bind my quilts. Many of the letters I received after being featured in a magazine requested my method for binding, leading me to believe that many quilters are stumped when it comes to finishing the scalloped edges of hexagon quilts. I have several ways of finishing uneven edges. Of course, the edges of the quilt can be trimmed straight before binding. There should be a line of quilting or basting to keep the edges from stretching.

I often use purchased bias tape for binding. Most quilts will need four 3-yard packages. Use single fold tape and place it face down on the outer row of hexagons. Sew, following the angle of each piece. At the outside corners, hold the binding loose, rather than making a pleat. At the inside corners, just pivot and continue sewing. The other fold of the tape is brought to the back of the quilt and whipstitched in place.

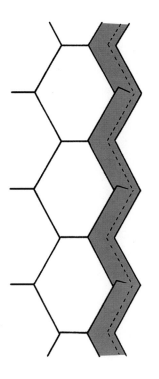

To make your own bias binding, cut 1 inch wide bias strips from the fabric. Press under one edge 1/4 inch. Sew the flat edge of the binding to each side of the quilt. Bring the fold to the back and whipstitch in place.

For quilts with straight edges, I use binding cut on the lengthwise grain of the fabric. Cut four pieces the same length as the sides of the quilt and 2 or 2 1/2 inches wide. (If you don't have a long piece of fabric, cut shorter pieces and seam together.) Sew to each side of the quilt. Overlap the binding at each corner and handstitch in place. Using a striped fabric, as I did in Enchanted Horizons (page 32), is very effective.

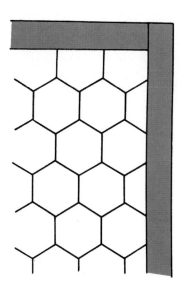

An original method for binding hexagon quilts is actually more like a facing. I like it because the quilt keeps its scalloped look.

Cut hexagons the same size, color and number as the outer row in the quilt. Sew the sides of the hexagons together, following the shape of the quilt.

Sew the joined hexagons to the quilt, with right sides together, by hand or machine. Trim the excess batting and backing and clip at the inside corners. Bring the hexagons to the back. Turn under a seam allowance and stitch in place. (In the quilt directions, I have listed the number and amounts for this method on several of the quilts with scalloped edges, even if they were finished with a different method.)

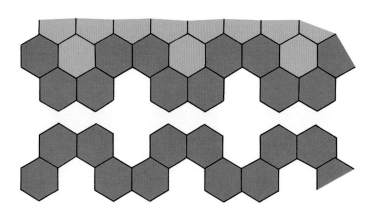

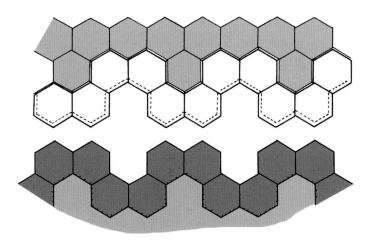

DESIGNING WITH HEXAGONS

If the term "designing quilts" is intimidating to you, just think of it as "flower arranging"! I started creating my first quilts by looking at the scenery during our many years and many more miles of travel. I also obtain ideas from other quilts. Combining ideas from many different quilts, I add and subtract until I create a whole new look.

Hexagon graph paper also helps in designing. As you color in various arrangements of the hexagons, others will appear to you. You'll achieve different effects with the points of the hexagon vertical rather than horizontal.

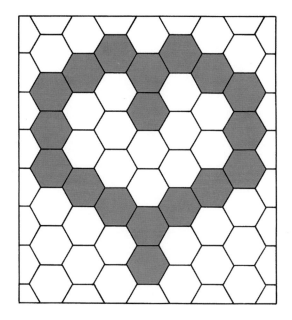

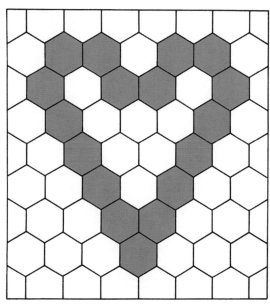

The graph paper also helps in designing the pictorial quilts. Use a children's coloring book and transfer a picture with carbon paper onto the graph paper. Draw around the hexagons closest to the transferred design. The smaller the hexagon, the more detailed the design can be.

Recently I have enjoyed using a design wall. This is a piece of white flannel fabric mounted on a board on the wall. It has a square grid drawn on it to help me keep the rows straight. The cut hexagons stick to the flannel and I can rearrange or replace them until I'm satisfied with the design.

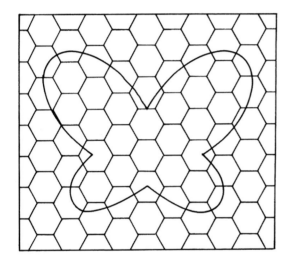

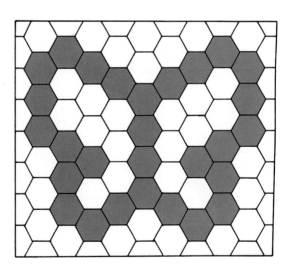

Garden Party

DRAFTING THE HEXAGON

Although I have included pattern pieces in several sizes, you may want to draft your own size for a project. Perhaps you have a wonderful floral print but each flower is exactly 1 1/4 inches across. To use a 1 inch hexagon would cut off the tips of the petals and the 1 1/2 inch hexagons would be too large. You'll find the hexagon is both fun and easy to draft.

Using a compass with pencil, draw a circle on a piece of plain paper. Keeping the compass at the same setting, which is the radius of the circle, place the point on the line and make a mark across the line with the pencil. Move the point of the compass to the mark and draw another mark on the circle. Continue to do this until the pencil is on the first mark. This evenly divides the circle into six sections. Using a ruler and sharp pencil, draw lines from mark to mark (place the ruler exactly where the marks cross the circle).

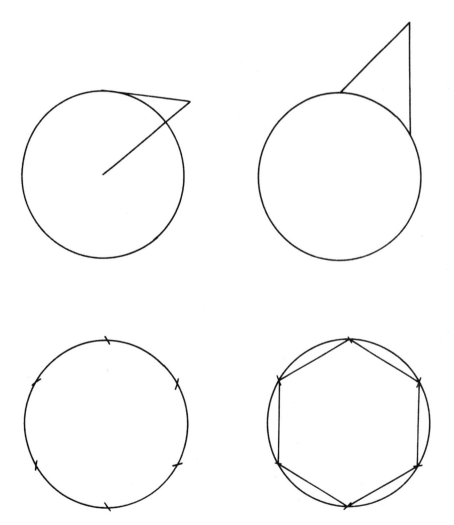

To enlarge or reduce the size of the hexagon, draw lines from the center to the points and beyond. Use a ruler to draw the outside lines of the desired size of hexagon.

The hexagon can be further divided into the other shapes. Drawing lines connecting the opposite points creates the small triangles that can be used with the hexagon. Erasing every other line radiating from the center yields the diamond.

The drafted hexagon, triangle, and diamond are the finished size. Add seam allowances to each shape.

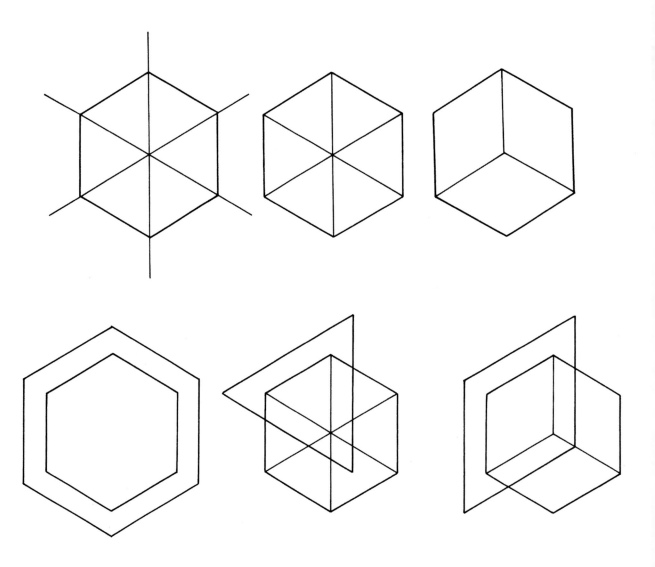

Garden Party

Patterns

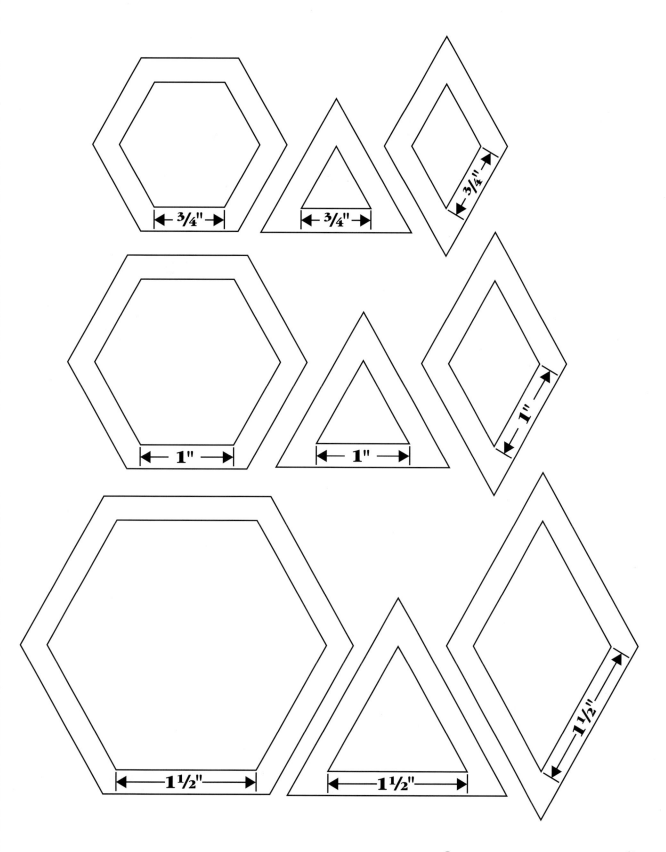

HEXAGON GRAPHS

Garden Party

Garden Party

$\mathcal{S}$OURCES

Plexiglass templates for use with rotary cutters are available in sets of three sizes (3/4", 1", 1 1/2"). Each template is clear with etched 1/4" seam lines. Send $11.95 plus $2.00 for postage to:

First Star
10237 East Rio de Oro
Tucson, Arizona 85749
(520) 885-7278

ABOUT THE AUTHOR

Dorothy Kinsley Wray, a native of Kansas, has been making hexagons quilts since the early 1970's. Her fascination with hexagons began when, after retiring, she made a Grandmother's Flower Garden as her first quilt. More than one hundred hexagon quilts later, she continues to explore the potential of that six-sided shape.

Dorothy has been featured in several magazines and has shown her quilts throughout the United States. This maker of so many Grandmother's Flower Garden quilts is not only a grandmother, but a great-grandmother. After residing in California and Arizona for many years, Dorothy and her husband Robert have settled in Citrus Heights, California.

First Star

Celebrating the grand traditions of quiltmaking

Nine Patch Wonders
Blanche Young and Helen Frost

Patches of Glory: An Americana Sampler
Deborah Gordon

Country Lanes
Blanche Young

Sweet Dreams: Heirloom Quilts for Babies
Deborah Gordon and Helen Frost

Whig Rose Star
Helen Frost

Corn & Beans and other Country Quilts
Deborah Gordon

First Star
10237 East Rio de Oro
Tucson, Arizona 85749
(520) 885-7278